With love
from

_____

to

_____

LITTLE ☆ STARS™

LEO

A parent's guide to the little star of the family

JOHN ASTROP

with illustrations by the author

ELEMENT

Shaftesbury, Dorset ● Rockport, Massachusetts
Brisbane, Queensland

© John Astrop 1994

Published in Great Britain in 1994 by
Element Books Ltd.
Longmead, Shaftesbury, Dorset

Published in the USA in 1994 by
Element, Inc.
42 Broadway, Rockport, MA 01966

Published in Australia in 1994 by
Element Books Ltd.
for Jacaranda Wiley Ltd.
33 Park Road, Milton, Brisbane, 4064

Printed and bound in Great Britain by
BPC Paulton Books Ltd.

British Library Cataloguing in Publication
data available

Library of Congress Cataloguing in publication
data available

ISBN 1-85230-541-X

CONTENTS

THE TWELVE SIGNS

Everyone knows a little about the twelve sun signs. It's the easiest way to approach real astrology without going to the trouble of casting up a chart for the exact time of birth. You won't learn everything about a person with the sun sign but you'll know a lot more than if you just use observation and guesswork. The sun is in roughly the same sign and degree of the zodiac at the same time every year. It's a nice astronomical event that doesn't need calculating. So if you're born between

May 22 and June 21 you'll be pretty sure you're a Gemini; between June 22 and July 23 then you're a Cancer and so on. Many people say how can you divide the human race into twelve sections and are there only twelve different types. Well for a start most people make assessments and judgements on their fellow humans with far smaller groups than that. Rich and poor, educated and non-educated, town girl, country boy, etc. Even with these very simple pigeon holes we can combine to make 'Rich educated town boy' and 'poor non-educated country girl'. We try to get as much information as we can about the others that we make relationships with through life. Astrology as a way of describing and understanding others is unsurpassed. Take the traditional meaning of the twelve signs:

Aries - is self-assertive, brave, energetic and pioneering.

Taurus - is careful, possessive, values material things, is able to build and make things grow.

Gemini - is bright-minded, curious, communicative and versatile.

Cancer - is sensitive, family orientated, protective and caring.

Leo - is creative, dramatic, a leader, showy and generous.

Virgo - is organised, critical, perfectionist and practical.

Libra - is balanced, diplomatic, harmonious, sociable, and likes beautiful things.

Scorpio - is strong-willed, magnetic, powerful, extreme, determined and recuperative.

Sagittarius - is adventurous, philosophical, far-thinking, blunt, truth-seeking.

Capricorn - is cautious, responsible, patient, persistent and ambitious.

Aquarius - is rebellious, unorthodox, humanitarian, idealistic, a fighter of good causes.

Pisces - is sensitive, imaginative, caring, visionary and sacrificing.

If you can find anyone in your circle of friends and acquaintances who isn't described pretty neatly by one of the above it would be surprising. Put the twelve signs into different lives and occupations and you see how it works. A Taurean priest would be more likely to devote his life to looking after the physical and material needs of his church members, feeding the poor, setting up charities. A Virgoan bank robber would plan meticulously and never commit spontaneous crimes. A Leo teacher would make learning an entertainment and a pleasure for her pupils.

So with parents and children. A Capricorn child handles the business of growing up and learning in a very different way to a Libran child. A Scorpio parent manages the family quite differently to an Aquarian. The old boast, 'I'm very fair, I treat all my children the same', may not be the best way to help your little ones at all. Our individual drive is the key to making a success of life. The time when we need the most acceptance of the way we are is in childhood. As a parent it's good to know the ways in which our little ones are like us but we must never forget the ways in which they are different.

LITTLE LEO

Roll out the red carpet, strike up the fanfares and down on one knee. Royalty has come to stay! This little Prince Charming who thinks he's the cat's whiskers is allowing you to become the leading figures in his court. Perhaps it's a tiny princess waiting for the rose petals to be strewn before she tiptoes her dainty little feet across your living room carpet. Either kind, you've got some fun ahead. Little Leos come into this world expecting the best and just so that they get it, they bring sunshine, happiness, generosity and a lifetime of entertainment. When they get what they want, the three a's – appreciation, admiration, and affection, then they're the most lovable little beasts to have around. When they don't... the reaction is dramatic and the roars and growls from this little lion are intolerable. Once these cubs have been taught that respecting the needs of others is the way to get the respect they require themselves, you have one of the most affectionate, amusing and playful little characters to live with. Rarely content to take a back seat, you'll soon find

your small Leo in the middle of the gang handing out orders. They take over anything and everything as if they were made just to be in charge. If they've had a little help from sensitive parents who know what power lurks beneath the surface, they'll

be fair, they'll be popular, but they'll always be boss. If they don't get the guidance and are left to their own devices, another pushy bully takes over. The Leo sense of performance is prematurely developed, making them laugh a little louder, act the clown a little more frequently, and overplay dramatically the hurts and affronts that occur. The Leo power to see in the mind what they would like to make happen is there from the earliest years. Highly creative, they need encouragement and a constant flow of stimulating materials with which to carry out big thinking projects. It isn't all work, work, work by any means though, and at times you'll come face to face with the lazy lion who won't lift a finger to help in the house or even to help themselves. All parents of Leos will at some time feel they are just there to await the whims of these regal layabouts. It's strange how often this occurs when it's their turn for the menial chores around the house. You'll maybe have to settle in the end with offering the higher status tasks to her majesty if you want any help at all.

Sociable in the extreme, little Leos will be on their best behaviour when guests call, handing round sandwiches and drinks and taking over your role as host or hostess at the drop of a hat or a knock on the door. Although sometimes bossy amongst their contemporaries, lions are generous in the extreme, finding it easy to lend favourite toys to friends and sharing pocket money with hard up chums. When this gets a little extreme it can often be read as just Leo showing off, but the result is nevertheless generosity. Hardly a bad fault!

THE BABY

Your little Leo babe will settle easily into a good regular schedule but if the service is lacking the whole world will know it. A Leo baby's scream is an order not a plea. Mostly it's just to get a little attention when the exploration of fingers and toes has become a bore. Revelling in family occasions, they can take any amount of Grannies, Gramps,

Uncles and Aunts peering adoringly into the crib, beaming back sunshine with the glow of a beloved emperor surveying his court. From this moment on the pattern of a Leo life is set. Once a taste of this kind of attention has been enjoyed, the switching off moments will become trials. Sitting out the indignant yells when you decide enough is enough, now's the time for sleep, may find you having to be a little firmer than you would have wished. Leo babes want the fun and games to last forever. If they cry a little louder and longer than most, they also laugh, chuckle and spread a little more sunshine than most. Not a bad deal! Responsive to your every reaction they will always give encores for each new trick they learn – smiles, heaving themselves up on an elbow or the first mouthing of 'mama'.

THE FIRST THREE YEARS

Holding his almost empty dish aloft for you to applaud, with his face covered in half of his lunch and the rest on the floor, your little lion will master the art of feeding himself as long as you're around to watch and appreciate his skill. It may take a while before little Leo gets more than half of the food on the inside of him but to take back the task of feeding will be an affront to the lion cub's dignity and the screams of hurt pride will reverberate. The crawling bit is not a Leo favourite and once they've mastered that rather humble form of transport it's no time at all before they are on their feet. Adventurous and curious, little Leo will try out her talents on anything and everything. This will be the time for moving the delicate, the dangerous and the precious. Heaven help you if you try to get things away from the small but emphatic grasp once they've been commandeered. Diversion tactics are better than showing these little superstars that you don't trust them with whatever. A lot of the Leo tantrums and tears will be for effect. In fact they are quite brave little characters and often, after quite a hard fall, little Leo will look around to see if anyone saw and – finding no potential audience – trot off without wasting a good scream. The sheer creativity of this small performer  begins to blossom around the third year and the home will ring to song, dance, playacting, and surprisingly good mimicry of anything that will get you giggling. OK, you know by now that you've got a little show-off in the family, but only with the best intentions. Leos want to be happy but they also want everyone else to be happy and that takes a lot of learning and they just need to start early.

THE KINDERGARTEN

Being sociable little beasts the lion cubs love the chance to try out their leadership potential on a crowd. The early days may find a few other Moms complaining that your little one is riding somewhat roughshod over their little pets – getting there first, grabbing the biggest, being the loudest, organising everyone, and boasting. Nursery school is too great a temptation for your little Leo. It hits them just at the time they discover that biggest is best

18

and they never look back. 'Our car's fastest', 'My dad's bigger than yours'; it'll take some subtle help just to steer your little darling away from being a bit of a bully without realising it. Small lions take to a good heart-to-heart as long as they don't lose face and are made to look silly. After all, they only want to please and if they can do that by becoming a model of generosity and good behaviour the sacrifice could be worth it.

SCHOOL AND ONWARDS

Leos are a godsend to teachers in the first days of a brand new class. Their enthusiasm and confidence are a help and encouragement to the more timid classmates and the desire to join in and be good at everything sets some healthy competition going. They love school, for every day there is a chance to shine in one thing or another. You'll have to make time after school for the grand viewing of creative works that are small enough to be transportable (they always love painting bigger than anyone else), the recounting of achievements and the enacting of the major events. Through the years, though interest in some subjects may wane and an occasional lapse of a few months into Leo laziness may occur, little Leo will be a good achiever as much for her own pride as yours. Extra school activities, drama, dance, sport and games, will be enthusiastically supported. Be there Mom!

THE THREE DIFFERENT
TYPES OF LEO

THE DECANATES

Astrology traditionally divides each of the signs into three equal parts of ten degrees called the decanates. These give a slightly different quality to the sign depending on whether the child is born in the first, second or third ten days of the thirty-day period when one is in a sign. Each third is ruled by one of the three signs in the same element. Leo is a Fire sign and the three Fire signs are Leo, Sagittarius and Aries. The nature of Fire signs is basically creative so the following three types each has a different way of expressing their creative abilities.

First Decanate - July 24 to August 2

This is the part of Leo that is most typical of the sign qualities. The Creative Performer. The need to bring into being the things they so clearly visualise is the basic drive of this decanate of the most creative of all the signs. From the earliest years these Leos have the ability to invent games that become a reality for their little friends. This talent makes for great popularity which they take for granted as their natural right. Later in life this will manifest as an appreciation of a sense of power over others, to amuse, to entertain, or even to control. A lot find their way into politics where their personality gets them elected almost regardless of their policies. However successful they eventually become in the great world outside, Leos remain essentially family orientated, seeing in their closest ones the real essence of meaning in their lives and devoting much care and pride to developing the talents of their own young ones. From the first ten days come many who make their mark on the masses in a much more powerful way than through entertainment. Henry Ford made us mobile, Carl Jung got us looking inside ourselves, and Yves St Laurent made us look good.

Second Decanate - August 3 to August 12

This is the Adventurous Performer. Ruled by the benefic planet Jupiter and sharing some of the far-ranging qualities of Sagittarius, these Leos never stop their search for improvement in whatever field they pursue. They are great travellers both physically and mentally and many are innovators in that they explore new areas and ideas that have previously been ignored. They require less reassurance than the previous decanate, being prepared to go out on a limb in their search for truth. Sir Alexander Fleming, the discoverer of penicillin, and space traveller Neil Armstrong typify this part of Leo. Grandma Moses, although a late starter, made her mark worldwide as a naive artist. The outrageous Andy Warhol held his court like a true Leo of this decanate.

Third Decanate - August 13 to August 23

This is the Self-willed Performer. Ruled by the energetic planet Mars and sharing some of the go-it-alone qualities of Aries, these characters are always different. One of a kind! They are far more impetuous, prepared to gamble, and often will go way over the top in any area where they feel confident. The pioneering influence of Aries makes them less vulnerable to the need for constant acclaim and appreciation and for this reason they are freer to take risks in whatever activity they choose. Napoleon Bonaparte, Wild Annie Oakley, Lawrence of Arabia, each have their own unique 'loner' quality. Even Princess Anne maintains a 'do my own thing and say what I think' attitude although part of a close-knit royal family. If we're talking over the top, Mae West in her time was thought to be outrageous, but even she seems to be surpassed by the controversial Madonna.

OTHER LITTLE LEOS

Mums and Dads like you delighted in bringing up the following little performers. Yours will probably turn out to be even more famous!

First Decanate Leo

George Bernard Shaw, Mick Jagger, Susan George, Henry Ford, Jacqueline Onassis, Carl Jung, Robert Graves, Benito Mussolini, Emily Brontë, Yves St Laurent, Stanley Kubrick, Raymond Chandler, Peter Bogdanovich, Geraldine Chaplin.

Second Decanate Leo

Henry V of England, Guy de Maupassant, Dustin Hoffman, Lucille Ball, Robert Mitchum, Mary Shelley, Neil Armstrong, Grandma Moses, John Huston, Tony Bennett, The Queen Mother, Andy Warhol, Melanie Griffith, Sir Alexander Fleming, Whitney Houston.

Third Decanate Leo

Alex Haley, Annie Oakley, Alfred Hitchcock, Napoleon Bonaparte, George Shearing, Robert de Niro, T.E. Lawrence, Coco Chanel, Princess Anne, Steve Martin, Claude Debussy, Ogden Nash, John Lee Hooker, Robert Redford, Patrick Swayze, Mae West, Madonna, Princess Margaret.

And Now the
Parents

THE ARIES PARENT

The good news!

This is a relationship of fire, enthusiasm, and super-creative activity with a dash of healthy competition thrown in for good measure. Big winner and little boss. Aries will soon sense, support and enthusiastically encourage little Leo's obvious leadership potential. Lion cubs learn easily; with a natural sense of creative self-expression and backed with liberal doses of appreciation they can push on to great heights. The Aries parent will delight in young Leo's firm independence and the sunny

good-natured bossi-
ness that automatically
makes any little Lion
the head of the gang
with young contempo-
raries. Leos will often
need help, however,
and possibly some sub-
tle restraint in this

'taking over' talent, for the popularity can turn to
resentment. Getting the balance right may be a
continual task for an Aries Mom or Dad as the pain
of an overthrown tyrannical dictator can be incon-
solable. With a great sense of drama and an
irresistible urge to 'show off' (showbiz is full of
Leos) they need a good audience, but a firm Aries
parent can help them learn when enough is
enough. There can be no open combat, though, for
Ram and Lion are hotheads, neither easily admit-
ting defeat. Too many chiefs, too few warriors,

smoke peacepipe, heaps better fun. For all the Leonine natural confidence there is a small requirement that they need in large doses – appreciation. They work best in areas where there is an immediate response to their achievements and will care little for modest backroom work that goes unnoticed. If the two of you work together on projects harmoniously, little Leo will learn the pleasure of giving appreciation as well as receiving it. Best activities to share with a big-thinking little Lion would be making things, planning things, painting huge pictures, singing, dancing, play acting and organising everybody.

...and now the bad news!

Let's face it, you're both hotheads, both fire signs, and both will think you know best. This has to see a few role reversals in day to day activity. Aries Mom or Dad can get just a little over the top in competitive issues and your little Leo lads and lasses can get too big for their boots. There can be the most serious clashes with tempers fraying at the edges continually. Little Lions need someone to admire and finding a beloved parent dropping their dignity just to win a battle won't do the relationship a bit of good. If anyone can help these entertaining characters on the tough path to being somewhere well-respected and well in the public eye it is you! Don't blow it on a 'who's best' battleground. You're made to revel in each other's prowess. Enjoy!

THE TAURUS PARENT

The good news!

The Taurean parent has endless patience, and is rarely bored with the day-to-day routine of caring for home and loved ones. Generous little Leo brings more than a fair share of sparkle and sunshine to this relatively easy relationship. Lion cubs learn to deal with their own extrovert leadership potential by looking up to and emulating those for whom they can develop respect. Taurus, calm and secure, can fit the bill well. There is however a natural instinct for little Leos to take advantage of anyone who starts in on the role of servant. These regal youngsters can, if not stopped in their tracks at a fairly early age, push even the calm, ever providing, Taurean to the limit. Both of you are good, generous entertainers and it is in this area that you can help your little Lion get the right balance of thoughtfulness and leadership that will stand him in good stead later. Your little king or queen will enjoy helping to prepare for visits from little friends, organising snacks and games, and even serving their chums with fruit juice and cookies. Never forget though, the little vote of thanks and

comment on how well this task was done is much more important to your Leo child than to you. Leos respond to sincere appreciation and usually work hard to earn it, but the desire

for the limelight may, without a little injection of Taurean common sense, get out of hand. Plenty of creative activity is a productive safety-valve for these self-expressive children and Taurean patience in this direction will be richly rewarded. To create something out of nothing is the real Leo talent, the ability to see things clearly before they are created is always there and the tiniest Lions will surprise you with their 'big-thinking' plans. Add to this tangible stimulation in the form of musical instruments, paper, paints, an old typewriter, you name it, and little Leo can become your Leonardo.

...and now the bad news!

Your easy-going attitude to life can be somewhat stretched if you expect little Leo to be a good sensible, down-to-earth character like you. What makes your life run so well is good routine and attention to detail and you could make a big mistake if you believe that this will work with King Leo. Details are a bore! When you have visualised the biggest of big plans, nobody in their right minds would expect you to fiddle and tiddle with the fussy  details. Little Leo won't put the newspaper down first before painting the Sistine chapel ceiling in her nursery. She won't wash the brushes out either. You will just 'have' to rise to this constant challenge to all you hold dear. If you nag and insist that all is done with due care and consideration, then you'll have a frustrated little genius who'll end up not doing a thing. If you don't, you will become a nervous wreck. The balance has to be right. If you can make the chores an artistic challenge, you're half way there.

THE GEMINI PARENT

The good news!

No child is going to want for a stimulating and varied childhood with you around. Alternating between interested friend, strict authority, sparkling entertainer, learned professor and clown, the Gemini parent is good news for little Leo. Small Lion cubs are sunny, creative, optimistic and will respond well to the continually changing stimuli of this mercurial adult. Needing only a little encouragement and plenty of appreciation, these Leo leaders confidently push themselves into the limelight. Finding the happy medium between good self-expression and over-dramatic showing off is a knotty but worthy problem for the sharp-witted Gemini mind. Young Leo's true leadership strength lies in honest generosity and a sense of justice. The Gemini parent's broad understanding of the world can teach this child the importance of respecting other people's needs and motivations. Gemini's quick change of moods makes most

parent/child clashes short-lived. Your little Lion won't be quite so fast to drop an affront to his dignity and may need to growl in a corner or, even better, in his den. All Leos need a hideaway where they can go and lick their wounds after a family battle, however trivial.

...and now the bad news!

Two possible snags to this otherwise harmonious and busy relationship are, one, the Geminean tongue, and two, the Geminean mind. When it comes to witty backchat and snappy comebacks the Twins are unbeatable. It's all in fun, but does your little Lion know? The big-thinking Leo doesn't always get little nuances of repartee and if there's a chance that they might feel that they are being 'put down' then they'll take it. Any excuse for a Leonine drama! Junior's penchant for 'big scenes' in stress situations will find better release in good humour than sarcastic put-downs. Punctured pride drags out the performance. The other problem, the Gemini mind, can result in you producing too many ideas, too many alternatives, too many seductive projects that can send little Leo's head in a whirl. Hold your horses, only you can work on projects six at a time; keep it exciting, but keep it simple for your creative cub.

THE CANCER PARENT

The good news!

Soft, sensitive and caring where your adored offspring are concerned you will be a receptive audience, prompt, scriptwriter and stage-dresser to this sunny little performer. Leo is a natural leader and thrives on encouragement. Lion cubs can be bossy and overbearing with other children but their happy, playful disposition can rarely give offence. The Cancer parent will be aware that 'putting down' Leo's abilities for taking over anyone or anything is bound to produce a roar of hurt pride. An appeal to Leo's natural generosity will ensure that the others get a look in. The Cancer parent is a great homemaker and will need to keep open house for the string of buddies that little Leo will have to entertain. At least Junior will keep them amused. Cancers have a strongly developed sense of protectiveness and this can make them great worriers, conjuring up potential disasters and stepping in to avert them, just in case. Probably the whole human race survived only because of the large percentage of Cancerians protecting us all with their 'premonitions' and 'feelings'. However, you'll have to use more than a little low cunning if you're to protect brave little Leo. The first two or three times you do this you'll discover that

your little Lioness will have none of it if it makes her look as if she is unable to look after herself. Little Leos don't mind devoted servants doing things for them, but the implication that a big cat like them can't stand on their own two feet will be met with a roar of indignation, and you will be in the doghouse. A good balance between servant and protector can avoid your being a slave to a spoilt little horror and present you with a well-balanced offspring with a good self-reliant attitude that does you credit and helps him make friends and influence people.

...and now the bad news!

The eternal Cancerian problem is that they adore their children so much they spoil them. Unfortunately little Leos can be insatiable. Overindulge the luxury-loving Lion cub and you'll have a tyrannical monster on your hands, spoilt, snappy and ungrateful. Don't go to the other extreme though, and totally ignore little Leo's great need for attention, for you'll be met with, not a dignified lion, but a whining, approval-seeking pussycat. It's not a pretty sight when a small Leo doesn't get a little pat on the back for effort and is forced to go over the top to get attention. You've seen them making other mothers' lives a misery in the shopping mall. They probably aren't all Cancers and Leos but read this as typical of the dilemma and you're on the road to avoiding it. Back your own feeling and sensitivity as a good guide for hitting the middle road.

THE LEO PARENT

The good news!

This is a royal family and you above all should know the protocol. Bringing up the heir to the throne has been the duty of all kings and queens since the beginning of time and here's another little one just like you! For a Leo parent who has a good honest self-knowledge, this child should present no problems. There will be differences, of course, but the similar desire for recognition and need to think big will strike a familiar note. When you criticise Junior's arrogance and extravagance, you may first have to take the splinter from your own eye. Big Leo's ambitions for the child coupled with little Leo's ample self-confidence could conquer the world, and probably will. Along the way the Leo parent can help this youngster get that great leadership potential into perspective. All that coming out on top at the expense of little playmates can lead to rejection and hurt pride. However, generous to a fault, little Leos will share all possessions with their friends, and if this can extend to letting the others have a turn at being 'boss' so much the better. Strong characters like Leos need good role models when they're learning the trade, so to speak, and you'll be copied faithfully in both your good and bad

points – for what comes naturally to you will be equally easy for Junior. 'Do as I say and not as I do' is just not going to work here. The powerful Leo creativity should get a good boost in this parent/child relationship and working on big projects together will make more comfortable the sometimes aloof dignity that you both share. To be able to be proud of each other is a necessity for you both and what better than when you can work together as a team.

...and now the bad news!

As Leo Junior gets older there could be a little conflict as to who's king of the castle and without a liberal dose of good humour this could be a power struggle. Your reactions are going to be similar which is OK when enthusiasm rules, but if one of you thinks the other is taking over then hurt pride can cause over-dramatic situations that ruin the partnership. Pride has always had a bad press since the Victorians set about telling the world what to do – 'Pride has it's fall' etc – but the other positive side of Leo pride is represented in the artisan's pride in a perfect piece of work, never accepting second best. This is of course the only kind of pride that concerns you and your little colleague. A friendly joint-directorship has got to be the answer that wins every time. Great activities to share are plenty of games (to top each other in the nicest possible way and learn to lose, both of you!), dressing up and play acting, puppetry, and hoards of materials for big creative activity.

THE VIRGO PARENT

The good news!

When it comes to running a smooth, efficient and well provided for household no one can beat you, the Virgo perfectionist. You need to do everything to the very best of your ability and will rarely be comfortable putting off until tomorrow what you can do today. You are going to find that the arrival of a little Leo fireball into your calm pond will make more than a gentle ripple, if not a minor tidal wave. The Virgo parent of a Leo child will soon learn one fact of life: these two sun signs operate on entirely different planes and mutual understanding and tolerance are essential for happy coexistence. The Virgo mother or father is a stickler for accuracy whereas the Leo child can be hopelessly inept (or just plain uninterested) when it comes to the details. Virgo senior is sparing with praise and despises any form of arrogance or ostentation, whilst the young Lion simply can't exist without appreciation and approval in fairly generous doses. Virgo believes in modesty in all things including shows of affection, but little Leo needs plenty of loving hugs and cuddles for reassurance. As usual it befalls the parent to adapt, and seeing things through Junior's eyes can achieve a great deal. Out of this slightly oddly-matched pair, you the

Virgo parent have the quick wits and the inventive mind that can keep the two of you in blissful harmony – at least two-thirds of the time. Young Leo is a constant delight with her sunny personality, never a perfectionist in the same way as the Virgo parent but nevertheless taking a great pride in everything she does. All this immodest stuff is what makes the inspired leader, the excellent organiser and the admired performer and you've got all of these wrapped up in one little lovable Lion cub. A lot of the time you can just sit back and enjoy the show. This one's warm, enthusiastic approach will add plenty of good-natured fun to your life and will repay a few bitten fingernails when it comes to holding back on the desire to correct all of Junior's mistakes. Don't let all of this take you to the other extreme, however, for little Leo can learn and if the chores are made a big creative challenge you may be on to a good technique for getting some action in otherwise unleonine territory.

...and now the bad news!

Only the one above. The nagging! It's so irritating to be constantly surrounded by the debris of little Leo's creative projects all carried out without proper preparation. Oh dear! Encouragement rather than nagging, constructive help in preference to sharp criticism, can unobtrusively rectify the little Lion cub's 'weaknesses', with both parties kept happy. The more you keep things to a shared activity level the better. All Leos love play acting (Virgoans make good actors, too); painting (you'll need to help tidy up); board games of all kinds (a good introduction to detail).

THE LIBRA PARENT

The good news!

If you're a typical Libran you'll have just the right household for a little Leo to thrive in. You love company and there will always be a great coming and going of visitors to your happy home. What better for a small character that loves a built-in audience more than anything. From the earliest days little Lions observe the reaction to their abilities and achievements of those around them and perform accordingly. The more the merrier as far as this confident little one is concerned. Leo children are not, for the Libran parent, particularly difficult to bring up. Self-confident and extroverted, they are affectionate by nature and anxious to please their parents. However, unless shown from an early age that they can't always play king pin and that the world does not revolve round them alone, Lion cubs can become bombastic, self-centred animals. Librans are extremely considerate of others and can teach little Leo that even 'stars' sometimes have to share the bill. The close friendship of the Libran parent, only too ready to lend an ear to Leo Junior's exploits, provides the willing audience this youngster needs. Leo children demand respect and give theirs wholeheartedly to a parent they can look up to. Libra

will need to overcome the natural tendency to take the easy path of non-commitment, coming down firmly on the side of right or wrong. Young Leos are powerful stuff in the making and are helped with strong guidelines. The Libran parent nevertheless is scrupulously fair and, by meting out justice (without fail), can easily gain the devotion and respect of the little Lion.

...and now the bad news!

The Libra parent's strong desire for peace and harmony can lead them to spoil their children. The 'anything for a quiet life' attitude can result in Leo Junior getting away with murder. The old Libran cliché, seeing both sides of any situation, can, with such a strong little character, result in the habit of always seeing Junior's side and giving in when clashes occur. Once in a while is fine but the Libran love of the easy way out can produce the worst of little Leo's exploiting tendencies, taking advantage at every opportunity. If you get yourself into this 'soft touch' situation it will get more and more difficult to extricate yourself in later years. Much as Librans hate coming down forcibly and emphatically when decision-making this will have to be established early on in the game. Little Leo will push to the limit until a boundary is drawn. If you love harmony be tough sometimes and always appreciative of the notice that your Lion cub takes of what you say.

THE SCORPIO PARENT

The good news!

This relationship is the meeting of two power-ful spirits. Both you and your small Lion want to be in control. Little Leo's budding talent for organising will quickly challenge your confident 'I'm in charge' attitude to perfect parenting. No great problem for such a good natural psychologist; Scorpio's greatest pleasure is a challenge and if the challenge is a big one so much the better. Little Leo will be the perfect answer to this requirement, providing not only the challenge but the promise of great rewards. The great Scorpio temptation is that in the desire to bring out the best in their youngsters they will forcefully manipulate them. With weaker children this can be a great danger but not so with little Leo. The Leo child is ambitious, confident and

anxious to succeed. Backed by the sheer determination of a Scorpio parent with the knack of 'making things happen', there's nothing this enthusiastic little one can't achieve. Scorpio can quite literally be the 'power' behind the Leo 'throne'. These two signs working together will be a formidable partnership. The Scorpio's inherent psychological understanding will recognise little Leo's need for appreciation and be quick to give sincere support. Building self-confidence without excessive self-importance will be a task worthy of this intelligent parent. Little Leo's sense of fun and love of life is irrepressibly catching and Scorpio's natural wit will find easy response with this young partner. Being such a powerful parent, you will have to take care not to exceed your support role in order to get the best from little Leo and also make sure that you are pushing towards the child's dreams rather than you own.

...and now the bad news!

It's quite obvious that with such strong drives the two of you will get drawn into negative power struggles. At the end of a tough day, and even

Scorpios have 'em, tests of will between you can produce nothing but noisy dramatics and sullen showing off with no credit to either party. You both get hurt easily and take the pain deeply, so you would be wise to establish a pattern of defusing battle situations. Divert the energies at all costs and work together not against each other. Try to share some activity or outlet at which you are both good, but find one where the competitive element in both of you can take a back seat to fun and enjoyment.

THE SAGITTARIUS PARENT

The good news!

Sagittarians love their freedom like they loved their own childhood. In fact their sheer exuberance for life and adventure never really grew up at all; it just stayed on from childhood. This doesn't make them the best of parents if you're seeing the job conventionally. See it the Sagittarian way and you have something else. Their fair-minded attitude to children makes them popular, but in no way doting, mums and dads. Kids are pals: keep 'em healthy, keep 'em occupied, keep 'em friendly and keep 'em on the move. Fresh air and exercise tends to be the Sagittarian answer to their youngster's problems. That, with a good sense of fun, can keep most things on an even keel. The Leo child, though soon self-reliant, has a sensitive side that may react over-dramatically to Sagittarius's sometimes blunt, matter-of-fact manner but if ground rules are established early the worst of the Archer's honest criticisms may become acceptable to the proud little Lion. Little Lion cubs have to be loved and appreciated and if you point out a glaring fault you will have to reassure this one that you still think he's great anyway. This goes for the Sagittarian love

of teasing too. Fun is shared with enthusiasm, but if it's at his own expense the proud Lion may show little amusement. Although you may be enjoying the independence that your self-reliant small Lion allows you, there is a deep need for reassurance, though Junior's apparent confident showmanship may keep it hidden. By praising successes and consoling failures, Sagittarius can be a constant support for this young one's creative self-expression. Blessed with an excellent sense of proportion, the Archer can teach little Leo the difference between being a shining light and a boring 'show off'. This is potentially a lasting, good fun relationship of two of the fieriest of signs.

...and now the bad news

It's almost too rare to mention in this rather ideal combination of creative go-getters but very occasionally things can go wrong. The most likely problem will be Sagittarius just not being there when really needed, a little too often on the move to notice the tiny Leo's prowess. It'll happen rarely, but when it does, the worst fears of having a clinging demanding child to hamper the Archer's freedom may be realised. Nothing, however, that a little penance in the form of a couple of weeks of studied 'togetherness' can't rectify. Keep the chuckles going!

THE CAPRICORN PARENT

The good news!

Practical and conscientious, you have all the qualities that make a perfect parent. Capricornians offer their children great security, and firm but fair discipline. Praise will be given when it is deserved and not otherwise. The Leo child develops early confidence and self-reliance in a good atmosphere, but without constant reassurance can languish and become withdrawn. Here a fair balance should be struck. In the understanding that Leo needs a great deal more recognition and applause for achievements than you would find tasteful, you can at least hope to teach the young Lion the difference between true pride in achievement and sheer vanity. It will not be long before you discover that there are more great differences between the two of you. Cautious by nature, the Capricornian parent is thrifty, responsible and slow to venture on untrodden ground. In contrast the Leo child is a born spender in all senses. Small Lions throw themselves enthusiastically into untried but attractive projects with little thought given to, in your terms, the necessary details that guarantee success. No parent has more patience than the Capricorn for the task of

familiarising Junior with the 'nuts and bolts' side of life. Keep it subtle though, for these natural leaders won't always see themselves as having to care about menial tasks, their role in life being the creative big thinker and the planner. It has to be said that whatever you say about learning the basic rules and applying yourself to the dull tasks that ensure the success of any project, your little protégé will ignore all of this and still be successful. You're not wrong in your beliefs, you've just got the wrong material on which to prove the point. The rewards for taking this constant frustration on the chin are enormous. Being ambitious for yourself and your loved ones, you will be delighted to find that little Leo has the same idea but a different way of getting there. It's almost as if the confident sunny nature of your little Lion is enough to guarantee popularity and support without seeming to work for it at all. Maybe in the end you can forgive yourself for a little pride.

...and now the bad news!

'You shouldn't', 'you mustn't', and 'you can't', are the trap that all Capricorns can easily fall into with these sometimes wayward and always spontaneous bcings. You've just got to let your Lion cub take risks, follow brilliant ideas and explore sheer unabashed creativity in Leo's own unique way. It's extravagant and wasteful but the only way for them, and if the results are unnoticed and unappreciated by the one for whom they have the most respect, a gap will grow in your relationship that will be difficult to bridge.

THE AQUARIUS PARENT

The good news!

Gregarious Aquarius thrives on company and has a home that is usually filled with interesting, unusual visitors of every description at every opportunity. To the Leo child, born to be a star, if only a minor one, this provides a ready-made audience. Young Leo should flourish in the social activity that is part and parcel of the Aquarius parent's lifestyle. Both parent and child share a love of people, but whereas Aquarius prefers to mingle with the crowd and be part of the group, little Leo needs to come to the fore and take a special bow. A natural leader and performer, herein lies Leo's talent and also the main contrast with the Aquarian. This parent will need to accept young Leo's desire to stand out from the crowd and encourage self-expressive activities, at the same time spelling out the Aquarian truth that all human beings deserve respect and no man is superior to any other. If successful in treading the tightrope of developing modesty without squashing Leo's sense of uniqueness, the Aquarian will be well rewarded. One should also

bear in mind that Leo children need to express their warm feelings. The young fire sign hasn't the detachment of this parent and will indulge in occasional over-dramatic tearful outbursts; calm reasoning may help a little, but not as much as a big cuddle. Being opposite signs of the zodiac, Aquarius and Leo make a pretty complimentary pair as long as they are open to seeing the other's point of view. In fact this can help each other immensely. Aquarians do their own thing, caring little for what others think; Leos care a great deal what others think. If each gains a little from their relationship one could ideally expect a Leo not quite so vulnerable to criticism and an Aquarian not quite so oddball for the sake of being so.

...and now the bad news!

As mentioned above, the true Aquarian can be a little coldly detached. Often caring more for good causes and big general issues concerning humanity at large, the close one-to-one side of relationships can sometimes get neglected. Only a Leo knows when they feel neglected. You may think you spend all the time in the world with your demanding offspring but if it isn't enough you'll soon know about it. The Leo answer to lack of recognition is to try harder and harder and harder. In your terms this is just painful showing off and you'll have none of it. Read the signs early and share your causes with a little Lion for peace of mind.

THE PISCES PARENT

The good news!

To the ever-loving Pisces parent, young Leo can be a constant ray of sunshine embodying the very self-confidence that Fishes often lack and a potential for making real the fantasies of this imaginative parent. Little Leos take advantage of willing service more than any other, and positively lap up maternal or paternal doting. However, the Piscean's selfless attitude and ever-ready helping hand can change the proud Lion into a purring 'lazy cat' if overindulged. This natural tendency may be difficult to restrain but it is well worth the effort. Highly creative and energetic, young Leo responds well to an appreciative audience. Shared projects with plenty of imagination and vision that allow Junior to take the fore will build experience in handling the natural talent for leadership. Sensitive Pisces can teach the understanding of other people's feelings, preventing Leo's well meant exuberance from riding roughshod over less powerful playmates. Learning to give the others a 'turn' can be an important lesson in helping to

produce a just ruler rather than a bossy tyrant. Once this is sorted out the unchanging warm affection and grand achievements of big-hearted Leo will more than repay this parent's loving self-sacrifice. The closeness of this couple will be enhanced by the imaginative qualities that they inspire in each other. Projects shared will be positive if little Leo can develop natural organising abilities and be assisted in finding ways in which the boring tasks can be made more exciting and worth doing. Pisceans are rarely without a feeling for the more spiritual, unmaterialistic side of life and, although admiring little Lion's sheer get-up-and-go ambition, will introduce an appreciation of the great outdoors, the sun, the sky, the sea and the pleasure of being part of one great whole.

...and now the bad news!

Little Leo, with all that spontaneity and impulse,

is a handful to manage and will need some firm guidelines and discipline. The great Piscean disaster is that they find it hard to be consistently firm. If 'no' means 'maybe' and 'maybe' means 'OK' then the pressure that little Leo can apply will grow by leaps and bounds. Pisceans are known for their loving kindness but also pitied for ending up sacrificing their individuality to their own demanding children. Make no mistake, this is self-inflicted in the Piscean desire to always be seen as loving and caring. The old saying that one has to be cruel to be kind may in moderation have some relevance in this relationship.

ON THE CUSP

Many people whose children are born on the day the sun changes signs are not sure whether they come under one sign or another. Some say one is supposed to be a little bit of each but this is rarely true. Adjoining signs are very different to each other so checking up can make everything clear. The opposite table gives the exact Greenwich Mean Time (GMT) when the sun moves into Leo and when it leaves. Subtract or add the hours indicated below for your nearest big city.

AMSTERDAM	GMT + 01.00	MADRID	GMT + 01.00
ATHENS	GMT + 02.00	MELBOURNE	GMT + 10.00
BOMBAY	GMT + 05.30	MONTREAL	GMT - 05.00
CAIRO	GMT + 02.00	NEW YORK	GMT - 05.00
CALGARY	GMT - 07.00	PARIS	GMT + 01.00
CHICAGO	GMT - 06.00	ROME	GMT + 01.00
DURBAN	GMT + 02.00	S.FRANCISCO	GMT - 08.00
GIBRALTAR	GMT + 01.00	SYDNEY	GMT + 10.00
HOUSTON	GMT - 06.00	TOKYO	GMT + 09.00
LONDON	GMT 00.00	WELLINGTON	GMT + 12.00

DATE	ENTERS LEO	GMT	LEAVES LEO	GMT
1984	JUL 22	3.58 PM	AUG 22	11.00 PM
1985	JUL 22	9.37 PM	AUG 23	4.36 AM
1986	JUL 23	3.25 AM	AUG 23	10.26 AM
1987	JUL 23	9.06 AM	AUG 23	4.10 PM
1988	JUL 22	2.51 PM	AUG 22	9.54 PM
1989	JUL 22	8.46 PM	AUG 23	3.46 AM
1990	JUL 23	2.22 AM	AUG 23	9.21 AM
1991	JUL 23	8.11 AM	AUG 23	3.13 PM
1992	JUL 22	2.09 PM	AUG 22	9.10 PM
1993	JUL 22	7.51 PM	AUG 23	2.51 AM
1994	JUL 23	1.41 AM	AUG 23	8.44 AM
1995	JUL 23	7.30 AM	AUG 23	2.35 PM
1996	JUL 22	1.19 PM	AUG 22	8.23 PM
1997	JUL 22	7.16 PM	AUG 23	2.19 AM
1998	JUL 23	12.55 AM	AUG 23	7.59 AM
1999	JUL 23	6.44 AM	AUG 23	1.51 PM
2000	JUL 22	12.43 PM	AUG 22	7.49 PM
2001	JUL 22	6.27 PM	AUG 23	1.28 AM
2002	JUL 23	12.15 AM	AUG 23	7.17 AM
2003	JUL 23	6.04 AM	AUG 23	1.09 PM
2004	JUL 22	11.51 AM	AUG 22	6.54 PM

John Astrop is an astrologer and author, has written and illustrated over two hundred books for children, is a little Scorpio married to a little Cancerian artist, has one little Capricorn psychologist, one little Pisces songwriter, one little Virgo traveller and a little Aries rock guitarist. The cats are little Sagittarians.